The author used many research documents and websites to gather the information and statistics in this book. Where possible, we've used the most up-to-date statistics, and where necessary, the author has used averages or amalgamated data. Every effort has been made to ensure the accuracy of the information in the first edition of this book, published in 2022.

Here is a list of sources used for this book:

6–7   How many animals have you ever seen?
animals.mom.me/number-animals-earth-3994.html
worldatlas.com/articles/which-species-make-up-the-animal-kingdom.html
reducing-suffering.org/how-many-wild-animals-are-there/

8–9   What makes vertebrates different from invertebrates?
academic.oup.com/jmammal/article/99/1/1/4834091
reptile-database.reptarium.cz/
amphibiaweb.org/amphibian/speciesnums.html
sciencedaily.com/releases/2018/02/180206090658.htm
worldatlas.com/articles/how-many-species-of-fish-are-there.html
oceanservice.noaa.gov/facts/cold-blooded.html

10–11   Did you hatch from an egg?
academic.oup.com/jmammal/article/99/1/1/4834091
vetstreet.com/our-pet-experts/dolphins-7-surprising-facts
hiltonheadisland.com/10-little-known-facts-dolphins/
dolphins.org/kids_dolphin_facts
blog.csiro.au/quick-facts-marsupials/
sciencefocus.com/nature/why-do-wombats-do-cube-shaped-poos/
ucmp.berkeley.edu/mammal/monotreme.html

12–13   Where do wild land mammals live?
worldatlas.com/articles/what-animals-live-in-north-america.html
rainforests.mongabay.com/03mammals.htm
currentresults.com/Environment-Facts/Plants-Animals/number-of
  -species-native-to-australia.php
environment.gov.au/system/files/pages/2ee3f4a1-f130-465b-9c7a-79373680a067/files/nlsaw-2nd
  -complete.pdf
oceanwide-expeditions.com/blog/menageries-of-small-mammals-exist-in-antarctica-and-the-arctic
focusonnature.com/SouthAmericaMammalList.htm
savethekoala.com/about-koalas/koalas-diet-digestion/
savethekoala.com/about-koalas/frequently-asked-questions/

14–15   How many animals live in the sea?
ncbi.nlm.nih.gov/pmc/articles/PMC3160336/
oceanservice.noaa.gov/facts/ocean-species.html
nationalgeographic.com/animals/article/anglerfish-mating-rare-video-spd

16–17   How many kinds of animals can fly?
amnh.org/about/press-center/new-study-doubles-the-estimate-of-bird-species-in-the-world
doi.gov/blog/13-facts-about-bats
livescience.com/28272-bats.html
batcon.org/why-bats/bats-are/bats-are-important
theguardian.com/environment/2016/oct/27/swifts-spend-ten-months-a-year-entirely-airborne-study
  -reveals
si.edu/spotlight/buginfo/bugnos
guinnessworldrecords.com/world-records/384659-largest-moth-by-wing-span-surface-area

18–19   How many mammals still live in the wild?
animalmatters.org/facts/wildlife/
worldanimalprotection.us/our-work/animals-farming
uinr.ca/moose-facts/
nwf.org/Educational-Resources/Wildlife-Guide/Mammals/Moose
mentalfloss.com/article/59461/10-gigantic-facts-about-moose

20–21   What animals share our homes?
petfoodindustry.com/articles/5845-infographic-most-of-world-owns-pets-dogs-are-tops?utm
  _source=KnowledgeMarketing&utm_medium=Watt%20
qz.com/933227/one-nation-is-particularly-crazy-about-cats/
mapsofworld.com/world-top-ten/countries-with-most-pet-bird-population.html
statista.com/statistics/1238576/india-share-of-pets-owned/
statista.com/topics/1258/pets/
oldest.org/animals/parrots/
guinnessworldrecords.com/world-records/longest-goldfish

22–23   Which animals are among the most deadly to humans?
statista.com/statistics/448169/deadliest-creatures-in-the-world-by-number-of-human-deaths/
who.int/news-room/fact-sheets/detail/malaria
nationalgeographic.com/animals/invertebrates/facts/mosquitoes
nationalgeographic.com/animals/reptiles/facts/black-mamba
schistosomiasiscontrolinitiative.org/sch?gclid=EAIaIQobChMItLjs4Pf26QIVTOztCh1Y
  _QHCEAAYASAAEgJMFPD_BwE
worldatlas.com/articles/the-animals-that-kill-most-humans.html

24–25   How many animals have become extinct?
nationalgeographic.com/animals/prehistoric/
pbs.org/wgbh/evolution/extinction/massext/statement_03.html
amnh.org/shelf-life/six-extinctions
nature.com/scitable/knowledge/library/homo-erectus-a-bigger-smarter-97879043/
blog.helix.com/woolly-mammoth-de-exctinction/
livescience.com/24011-triceratops-facts.html
animals.howstuffworks.com/dinosaurs/triceratops.htm

26–27   Which animals are most in danger?
livescience.com/63196-rainforest-facts.html
ovoenergy.com/blog/ovo-foundation/61-facts-you-need-to-know-about-the-rainforest.html
nationalgeographic.com/animals/2019/06/hyacinth-macaw-egg-laundering-for-pet-trade/
wwf.panda.org/discover/our_focus/freshwater_practice/freshwater_inititiaves/river_dolphins
  _initiative/

28–29   What are the big questions we should ask ourselves?
nationalgeographic.co.uk/environment/2019/05/one-million-species-risk-extinction-un-report
  -warns
e360.yale.edu/digest/nearly-15-000-miles-of-new-roads-will-be-built-in-tiger-habitat-by-2050
  -study-finds
un.org/development/desa/en/news/population/world-population-prospects-2019.html
adama.com/en/media/events/international-events/world-population-day
unesco.org/new/en/natural-sciences/ioc-oceans/focus-areas/rio-20-ocean/blueprint-for-the
  -future-we-want/marine-pollution/facts-and-figures-on-marine-pollution/
sailorsforthesea.org/plastic-pollution
bats.org.uk/about-bats/why-bats-matter/bats-as-pollinators
fws.gov/midwest/endangered/mammals/inba/curriculum/Chapter9.pdf
fws.gov/midwest/endangered/mammals/inba/curriculum/
un.org/sustainabledevelopment/blog/2019/05/nature-decline-unprecedented-report/

Text copyright © 2022 by HarperCollins Publishers Ltd
Cover art and interior illustrations copyright © 2022 by Aaron Cushley
All rights reserved. Published in the United States by Crown Books for Young Readers, an
imprint of Random House Children's Books, a division of Penguin Random House LLC, New York.
Originally published by Red Shed, part of Farshore, an imprint of HarperCollins Publishers, London,
in 2022.
Crown and the colophon are registered trademarks of Penguin Random House LLC.

Visit us on the Web! rhcbooks.com
Educators and librarians, for a variety of teaching tools, visit us at RHTeachersLibrarians.com
Library of Congress Cataloging-in-Publication Data is available upon request.
ISBN 978-0-593-37235-7 (hardcover) — ISBN 978-0-593-37237-1 (ebook)

Project Consultant: Paul Lawston
MANUFACTURED IN ITALY
10 9 8 7 6 5 4 3 2 1
First American Edition
Random House Children's Books supports the First Amendment and celebrates the right to read.

Penguin Random House LLC supports copyright. Copyright fuels creativity, encourages diverse
voices, promotes free speech, and creates a vibrant culture. Thank you for buying an authorized
edition of this book and for complying with copyright laws by not reproducing, scanning, or
distributing any part in any form without permission. You are supporting writers and allowing
Penguin Random House to publish books for every reader.

Written by Miranda Smith

Illustrated by Aaron Cushley

IF THE WORLD WERE 100 ANIMALS

A Visual Guide to Earth's Amazing Creatures

CROWN BOOKS

FOR YOUNG READERS
New York

How many animals have you ever seen? Our world is teeming with them, in all shapes and sizes. Animals are everywhere—in water, on land, in the skies—and more are being discovered all the time. The total number of individual animals on Earth is believed to be around 20,000,000,000,000,000,000,000 or 20 quintillion or 20 billion billion.

A number that large is hard to picture, so let's imagine if the world consists of just 100 animals and they are divided into vertebrates and invertebrates. . . .

6
are vertebrates

Vertebrates have a backbone inside them that helps to support their body. You are a vertebrate, as are other mammals, as well as fish, amphibians, and reptiles.

94
are invertebrates

Invertebrates don't have a backbone and they are all cold-blooded. Some have a soft body, like worms or squid. Others, such as spiders and crabs, have a hard outer casing called an exoskeleton that protects their body like a suit of armor.

Some invertebrates are so small that they can only be seen through a microscope.

What makes vertebrates different from invertebrates?

In addition to having backbones, vertebrates also have skeletons and muscles that allow them to move around easily. Think about how hard it would be to jump up and down if you didn't have any bones or muscles in your legs!

There are five groups of vertebrates in the world today: mammals, birds, amphibians, reptiles, and fish. If you imagine there are only 100 vertebrates in the world, how many are in each of the five groups?

Birds and mammals are warm-blooded, which means they can regulate their body temperature. Some sweat or pant to cool off, while others have feathers or fur to keep them warm.

9
mammals

14
reptiles

23
birds

Reptiles, amphibians, and fish are cold-blooded.
They are unable to control their body heat so they
take on the temperature of their surroundings.
They do this by moving from sunny areas where they
can warm up to shaded patches where they can cool down.

11
amphibians

43
fish

moonfish

There is only one fully warm-blooded fish—
the moonfish—which circulates heated blood
through its body as it swims in the cold ocean.

Did you hatch from an egg? The answer is no!

Like most mammals, humans are placental. However, there are two groups of mammals that do things differently: marsupials and monotremes. Let's find out more about all these groups of mammals, and how many of each there would be if there were only 100 baby mammals in the world. . . .

Placental mammals—like you—grow in their mother's womb. They feed from a placenta until they are born live as small versions of their parents. Then they are nursed by their mother.

94
are placental

baby dolphin

Dolphins are born with a mustache! Whiskers on their upper jaw help them find their mother's milk. Their whiskers fall out when they are no longer needed.

baby wombat

Wombats have cube-shaped poop!

5

are marsupial

Marsupial young are born live but not fully developed. Then they crawl to a pouch on their mother's stomach, where they are nursed on their mother's milk.

1

is a monotreme

baby echidna

Monotremes are the only mammals that lay eggs, but they also feed their babies, called puggles, with their milk. There are only five species of monotremes—the duck-billed platypus and four species of echidna. They all live in Australia and New Guinea.

NORTH
AMERICA

Pacific Ocean

Atlantic Ocean

Where do wild land mammals live?

They live on every continent except Antarctica. Some have adapted to survive in frozen landscapes or high up on stormy mountains. Others have made their homes underground in hot deserts or in the trees of steamy rain forests. If you imagine there are only 100 wild land mammals left in the world, which continents are home to most of them?

Equator

Mammals are the only animals with body hair. It is made from tough keratin that traps warm air. This creates an insulating layer that keeps heat in when it is cold and protects the mammal from the hot sun.

SOUTH
AMERICA

5 live in Europe

53 live in Asia

6 live in Australia

17 live in Africa

Arctic Ocean

ASIA

EUROPE

AFRICA

Pacific Ocean

Pangolins are the only mammal in the world to be covered from head to toe in sharp scales.

pangolin

Indian Ocean

Equator

OCEANIA

koala

Each day adult koalas eat up to 1 pound of eucalyptus leaves and sleep for up to 22 hours.

Southern Ocean

ANTARCTICA

How many animals live in the sea?

The oceans cover a massive 71 percent of our planet's surface and are home to 17,000 known species. But scientists believe most sea creatures haven't been discovered yet! If there were only 100 animal species in the sea, how many are known and how many are still to be discovered?

krill

blue whale

9

are known

The sea is home to the largest animal ever to have lived on Earth—the near 100-foot-long blue whale. It in turn feeds on the smallest inhabitants, tiny crustaceans called krill.

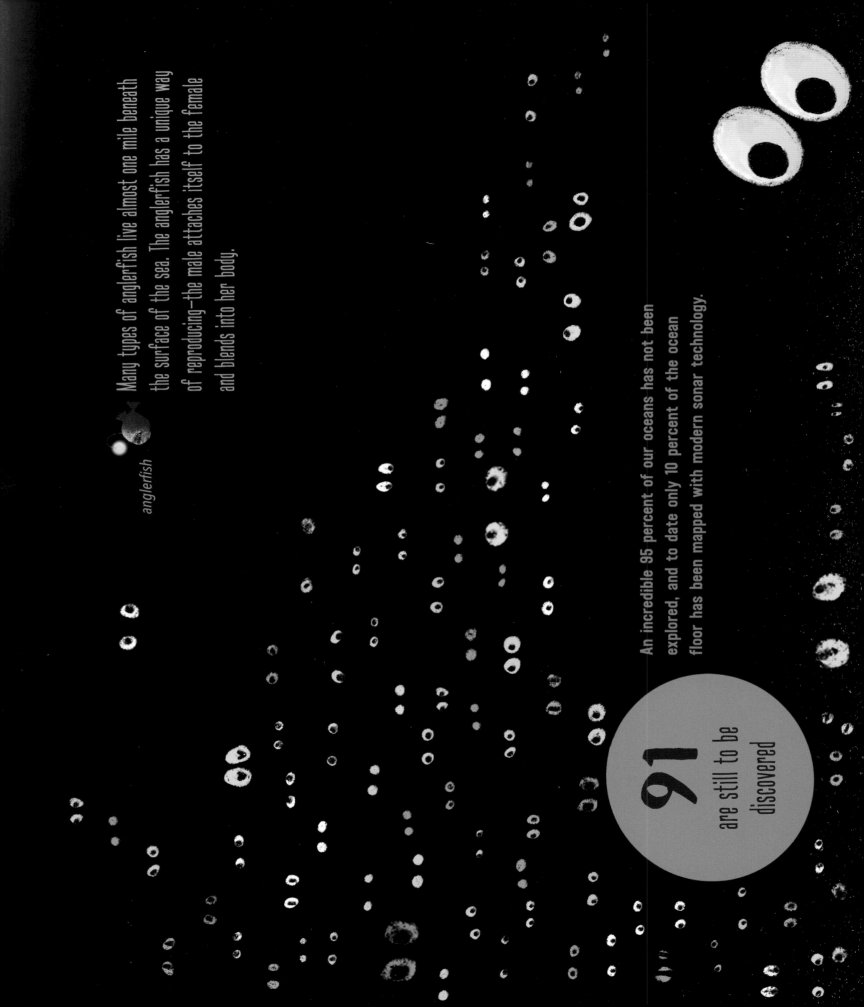

Many types of anglerfish live almost one mile beneath the surface of the sea. The anglerfish has a unique way of reproducing—the male attaches itself to the female and blends into her body.

anglerfish

An incredible 95 percent of our oceans has not been explored, and to date only 10 percent of the ocean floor has been mapped with modern sonar technology.

91

are still to be discovered

How many kinds of animals can fly? There are three types of creatures filling our skies—birds, bats, and insects. While most birds flap their wings to fly and soar and glide, bats can reshape their wings to turn and twist in the air. The way that the millions of different species of insects fly varies dramatically, from the bumbling bee to the darting dragonfly. If you imagine there are only 100 animals in the world that can fly, which are they?

2
are bats

Bats are the only mammals that can fly.

common swift

The common swift spends most of its life in the air, eating, mating, and even sleeping on the wing. Some stay airborne for up to ten months at a time!

4
are birds

94 are insects

The atlas moth is the largest moth in the world, with a wingspan of 11 inches.

atlas moth

How many mammals still live in the wild? Unfortunately, today very few mammals are wild. They are far outnumbered by humans and farm animals. People have been breeding animals for dairy, meat, transport, fur, and other uses for thousands of years. Sheep were the first domesticated animals, closely followed by pigs, horses, and cattle. So, if there were only 100 mammals in the entire world, how many of them would still be wild?

goats

sheep

5
live in the wild

moose

The name "moose" comes from a Native American word that means "twig eater." And they eat a lot of vegetation—up to 73 pounds a day in the summer!

36
are humans

horses

other large animals farmed for
their hides, milk, or meat

59
live on farms

beef cattle

pigs

Approximately 70 billion mammals
are farmed globally every year for meat,
milk, wool, fur, and hides. These animals
vary enormously, including all the ones
pictured on these pages.

dairy cattle

working animals

other small animals
farmed for their fur

What animals share our homes? Where people live in the world plays a big part in whether they have pets, how many, and what type of animal. If you imagine there are only 100 pets in the world, what types of animals are they?

33
are dogs

Dogs are most popular in the United States, where people spend more than $50 billion on their favorite pet dogs each year.

scarlet macaw

Scarlet macaws live a long time—one pet called Poncho reached the age of 92!

6
are birds

The largest number of pet birds are owned by people in Brazil.

A recent study of 52 countries found that Russians are the biggest cat lovers in the world.

23
are cats

12
are fish

The world's largest recorded goldfish was a whopping 18.6 inches long.

26
are other animals

In China, crickets housed in elaborate cages are popular pets.

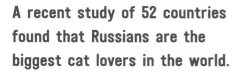

Which animals are among the most deadly to humans?

You probably think immediately of sharks and lions. In fact, sharks only kill around 8 people, and lions 20 people a year. The deadliest animal of all is a mosquito that carries the disease malaria and causes an astounding 750,000 human deaths every year. Many animals present a threat to people, so if you imagine there are only 100 deadly animals in the world, what might the others be?

81
are mosquitoes

There are over 3,000 species of mosquito, but the female Anopheles are the only ones known to carry and transmit malaria, which they do through biting and sucking blood.

The deadly East African black mamba is one of the fastest snakes in the world, slithering at over 12 and a half miles per hour, which is faster than most people can run.

East African black mamba

11 are snakes

4 are dogs

Most deaths are caused by stray dogs passing on a deadly disease called rabies through bites and scratches. Attacks by pet dogs are extremely rare.

Freshwater snails carry parasitic worms that infect people with a disease called schistosomiasis, killing more humans than sharks, lions, and wolves combined.

2 are freshwater snails

1 is a saltwater crocodile

The Australian saltwater crocodile is the largest reptile in the world and can measure up to 23 feet in length.

1 is a hippopotamus

The hippopotamus is one of Africa's most dangerous animals. It will attack anything that wanders into its territory.

How many animals have become extinct?

There are many, many more extinct animal species than those that are alive today. Fossils and bones help scientists to understand what these extraordinary creatures looked like, from the earliest life-forms through the dinosaur age to ice age giants such as the mammoth. If you imagine there had only ever been 100 animals, how many are extinct and how many are alive today?

10 are living

There are rings in the tusk of a woolly mammoth that, like the rings inside a tree trunk, tell scientists how old the animal was.

woolly mammoth skull

Triceratops skull

Triceratops was the size of an African elephant and had one of the largest heads of any land animal.

All that remains of the earliest prehistoric creatures are traces that include footprints, body impressions in rocks, and fossilized bones, as well as teeth, skin, nests, poop, and tracks. But that is enough to help scientists form a picture of what they looked like.

90 are extinct

Which animals are most in danger? Scientists say that every day dozens of animal species vanish forever. The Amazon rain forest is home to the greatest number and variety of animals, but many areas are being destroyed for logging and farming. If just one small area of rain forest is made up of 100 animals, what species, apart from untold insects, are lost when it is chopped down?

24
birds

54
fish

hyacinth macaw

For hyacinth macaws, it isn't just habitat loss that poses a threat to their survival but egg smuggling too. Poachers take the eggs from nests in the wild and smuggle them into other countries, usually on their bodies to keep them warm. On arrival, the eggs are hatched in captivity.

8
mammals

boto

The boto, or pink river dolphin, is in danger of disappearing because of the logging boats polluting the waters of the Amazon.

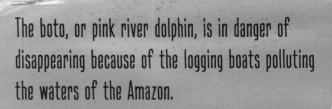

7
reptiles

7
amphibians

What are the big questions we should ask ourselves?

It is feared that by 2050 more than 1 million animal species that inhabit our planet today will be extinct, including the polar bear, rhinoceros, and gorilla. Climate change, pollution, deforestation, and overfishing are only some of the things people do that are putting our animals' world in danger.

By 2050, the global human population will have grown by at least a quarter. To house and feed everyone, huge amounts of land will have been cleared for buildings and farms. What can we do to stop the animals' habitats and ecosystems from being destroyed?

Today, up to 25,000 tigers are kept in zoos or as pets, but only 3,890 live in the wild across Asia. By 2050, more than 14,900 miles of new roads are planned to be built, which will destroy tiger habitats. How can we persuade the governments of these countries to change their plans?

By 2050, there will be more plastic than fish in the oceans. Once created, plastic lasts forever, breaking down into smaller particles called microplastics. These are dangerous for all living things in our seas, with more than 1 million seabirds and 100,000 marine mammals dying every year. What can we do to reduce our use of plastic and recycle plastic that already exists?

One half of all bat species could be extinct by 2050. More than 500 plant species, including banana, guava, and mango, rely on bats to pollinate their flowers, spread seeds, and control insects. Without bats in the rain forests, there may be no cacao trees and therefore no chocolate! How do we make people think about the connections between animals and the food on their plates?

When we imagine the world as just 100 animals, it is clear that we must all take action to ensure their survival. There are many ways that we can help. We can try to avoid using plastic and recycle what we do use. We can volunteer to clear our beaches, parks, and countryside of garbage. We can also help conservation organizations to save animals and their habitats. And we can write to our government representatives. As long as we all work together, we can make a real difference and save these animals before it's too late.

Wouldn't it be great if we could stop more animals from becoming extinct like the dodo? dodo